INTERVENTION

Phonics for
Older Students
BOOK 1

cvc, cvcc, ccvc, short, a, e, i, o, u
th, sh, st, long a, long e, end in y
ch, long i, long o, long u

The Science of Reading

ISBN: 979-8392340330

Phonics for Older Students – Level 1

Phonics for Older Students – Level 1

Research Based

Why Fluency?

To be considered "on level" in reading fluency, students should be able to read aloud an unrehearsed passage, (i.e., either narrative or expository, fiction or non-fiction that is 200 to 300 words in length) from a grade-level text, with at least 95% accuracy in word reading. As students read aloud, their reading should sound as effortless as if they were speaking (Hasbrouck & Glaser, 2012.) This does not come easily for some students, which is why fluency practice is so essential.

In order to be considered fluent readers, students in grades 9 through 12 should be able to correctly read 150 words per minute (Hasbrouck & Tindal, 2006). In 2006 and again in 2010, Hasbrouck and Hasbrouck and Tindal (respectively) put forth that "[i]t is sufficient for students to read unpracticed, grade-level text at the 50th percentile of oral reading fluency norms" and that "…teachers do not need to have students read faster because there is no evidence that reading faster than the 50th percentile increases comprehension." See chart below.

The best strategy for developing and improving reading fluency is to provide students with many opportunities to read the same passages orally several times. These exercises provide such opportunities. On each passage, there is space for reading fluency calculations. The best part is that the passages are quick and make it easy for students to read aloud repeatedly – and often – without taking up a lot of valuable classroom time. The activities can also be spread over several days.

Grade	Percentile	Fall WPM	Winter WPM	Spring WPM		Grade	Percentile	Fall WPM	Winter WPM	Spring WPM
1	90		81	111		5	90	166	182	194
	75		47	82			75	139	156	168
	50		23	53			50	110	127	139
	25		12	28			25	85	99	109
	10		6	15			10	61	74	83
2	90	106	125	142		6	90	177	195	204
	75	79	100	117			75	153	167	177
	50	51	72	89			50	127	140	150
	25	25	42	61			25	98	111	122
	10	11	18	31			10	68	82	93
3	90	128	146	162		7	90	180	192	202
	75	99	120	137			75	156	165	177
	50	71	92	107			50	128	136	150
	25	44	62	78			25	102	109	123
	10	21	36	48			10	79	88	98
4	90	145	166	180		8	90	185	199	199
	75	119	139	152			75	161	173	177
	50	94	112	123			50	133	146	151
	25	68	87	98			25	106	115	125
	10	45	61	72			10	77	84	97

These passages are Designed for older students who are very low readers.

This programs works for resource, whole class, RTI, and summer school. It can be used for centers, warm-ups, homework – anytime. If you are using this program with more than one student – partner up. Partnering students is engaging and lets everyone participate. I find that students helping students builds confidence and reinforces learning; additionally, by reading, tracking and reading again, student exposure to each passage is maximized. Research suggests that pairing readers with like-level reading partners is motivating and increases reading success.

Instruction for Group, Whole Class, or Zoom Fluency Practice

Before you begin, have a copy of one passage for each student. The PDF can be displayed before the whole class on a Smartboard or printed and projected on a document camera. As you explain the lessons, demonstrate what students will be doing.

Explain what fluency is - the rate and ease at which we read along with the flow of reading.

Break students into pairs and hand out one copy per student. If you are working with a group of students with varying abilities - pair like-leveled students together.

Explain the entire activity, as well as how to calculate combined words per minute, or CWPM. Then read the passage aloud. Have students track on their sheets as you read aloud. It is extremely beneficial for struggling students to hear the passage before they read it aloud. The goal isn't to have students stumble, but to optimize opportunities for ultimate success.

The first few times you do fluency as a class - the script below may be helpful:

1. **Check to make sure each person is in the right spot and then read the passage.**
2. **After you read the selected passage aloud, partner students and say something like:** *Put your name on your paper. Since you need to be marking your partner's paper, switch papers now. Raise your hand if you are Partner 1.*
3. **Pause until one student from each pair has their hand raised – acknowledge students when one person of each pair has their hand raised.**
4. **Raise your hand if you are Partner 2.** Pause until the other student from each pair has their hand raised – acknowledge students when the other partner has their hand raised.

   Excellent. When I say "Begin", all Partner 1s should quietly begin to read to their partners.

   All Partner 2s will use their pencils to keep track of their partner's errors. Partner 2s will put a line over each word pronounced incorrectly.

   When the timer goes off, all Partner 2s will circle the last word read, but Partner 1s will keep reading until the passage is complete. Does anyone have any questions?

5. Set the timer for two minutes. If there are no questions - *Begin.*
6. When the timer goes off: *Partner 2s, please mark your partner's score and give feedback to Partner 1s.*
7. **Walk around the room to make sure scores are being marked correctly.**
8. **Make sure students are ready and then switch for Partner 2s to read.**

   Ready? Begin.

Student: _____ Period: _____

Test 1 Date: _____ Test 2 Date: _____

Assessed for: _____ Letter Names _____ Letter sounds _____ Both

This assessment is designed to measure letter/name understanding as well as letter/sound correspondence.

Directions: Explain to your student what you expect either:

- I am going to point to a letter, and you are going to tell me what letter it is. *Do example 1.*

Record student answers below by putting a check by each letter a student gets correct.

Test: 1

Letter	Response	Letter	Response
x		c	
a		o	
b		g	
f		r	
e		n	
z		w	
p		t	
h		q	
j		i	
d		k	
v		y	
s		l	
u		m	

Test 2:

Letter	Response	Letter	Response
x		c	
a		o	
b		g	
f		r	
e		n	
z		w	
p		t	
h		q	
j		i	
d		k	
v		y	
s		l	
u		m	

Letters and Word Sounds

Example: P

Letter	Letter
x	c
a	o
b	g
f	r
e	n
z	w
p	t
h	q
j	i
d	k
v	y
s	l
u	m

Student: _____   Number: _____

Test 1 Date: _____   Test 2 Date: _____

Assessed for: _____ Letter Names   _____ Letter sounds   _____ Both

Phonics: CVC Vowel Pattern – Teacher Page

Word	Correct	Word	Correct
fun		rod	
at		set	
sit		sun	
met		sat	
pig		fin	
let		red	
mop		hit	
rat		mat	
fit		gum	
hid		hit	
pop		kid	
run		rug	
cat		ten	

Short "a" (5)	Short "e" (6)	Short "i" (5)	Short "o" (5)	Short "u" (5)

Phonics: CVC Vowel Pattern – Student Page

Word	Word
fun	rod
pat	set
sit	sun
met	sat
pig	fin
let	red
mop	hit
rat	mat
fit	gum
hid	hit
pop	kid
run	rug
cat	ten

fun   rod   pat

set   sit

ten   can   run

rug   met   sat   run

pig   fin   let

red   mop   hit   rat

mat   fit   gum

hid   hit   pop   kid

The cat sat.   3

The rat sat.   6

The cat and the rat sat.   12

The rat and the cat sat.   18

The cat and the rat sat on the mat.   27

The rat and the cat sat on the mat.   36

The cat sat on the hat.   42

The cat sat on the mat.   48

Was the hat on the mat?   54

The cat sat.   57

The rat sat   60

Name: _____ Number: _____

Phonics: CVC Vowel Pattern – Student Page

The bug sat.   3

The bug sat on the rug.   9

The bug went to the mug.   15

The mug was on the rug with the bug.   24

The bug was near a slug.   30

Is a slug a bug?   35

A slug is not a bug.   41

The bug and the slug sat on the rug.   50

A bug is a bug, but a slug is no bug.   60

The slug went from the rug.   66

The bug stayed near the mug   72

Words Read: _____ minus mistakes: _____ equals cwpm: _____

Phonics: CVC Short Pattern – Student Page

Pop had a mop.	4
Pop used the mop a lot.	10
Pop can hop with a mop.	16
Why did he hop with a mop?	23
Why did he mop a lot?	29
Pop will hop a lot.	34
Pop will hop with a mop.	40
Pop will hop with a mop.	46
Pop will hop on top of the bed.	54
Pop will set the mop down.	60
Pop can hop with a mop.	66

Words Read: _____ minus mistakes: _____equals cwpm: _____

Phonics: CVC Short Pattern – Student Page

It is fun to run.	5
It is fun to run in the sun.	13
Pop likes the sun.	17
Pop likes to run in the sun.	24
Pop can run.	27
Pop can run in the sun.	33
I can run in the sun.	39
Pop and I can run in the sun.	47
It is fun to run in the sun.	55
It is fun to run in the sun with Pop.	65
We like to run in the sun.	72

Words Read: _____ minus mistakes: _____equals cwpm: _____

Phonics: CVC Short Pattern – Student Page

The pig hid from Sid.	5
The pig had a bib.	10
The pig hid by the kid.	16
The kid hid the pig from Sid.	23
Sid sat by the kid.	28
Sid sat near the pig.	33
The pig hid.	36
Sid did not see the pig.	42
Sid did not see the pig with the bib.	51
Sid asked the kid for the pig.	58
Sid and the kid saw the pig.	65
Sid and the kid saw the pig with the bid.	75

Words Read: _____   minus mistakes: _____ equals cwpm: _____

Name: _____ Number: _____

Phonics: CVC Short Pattern – Student Page 1

Sid was a kid with a pig. Sid and his pig lived on	13
the top of a big hill. Sid and his pig liked to run.	26
Sid and his pig liked to run in the sun.	36
"It is fun to run in the sun," said Sid.	46
"Oink," said the pig. Pigs can't talk. Pigs can't	55
talk, but pigs can hop. Pigs can also run.	64
The pig was tan. The tan pig had red spots. It	75
was a hopping tan and red pig.	82
The tan and red pig hid from hopping Sid. Sid	92
found the tan and red pig. They hopped up the big	103
hill and went home.	107

Words Read: _____
minus mistakes: _____
equals cwpm: _____

Phonics: CVC Short Pattern - Student Page 2

Meg's dad has a tan van. Meg's dad has a | 10

red jet. Meg and her dad drove the tan van. Meg | 21

and her dad drove the tan van to the jet. | 31

It was raining. The jet was wet. The red jet | 41

was wet. Meg and her dad dried it with a rag. It | 53

was a big rag. | 57

Dad let Meg fly in the jet. Dad flew with | 67

Meg. The jet went up. The jet went up towards | 77

the sun. The jet ride was fun. | 84

After the jet, they hit the van and went | 93

home. Meg and her dad had a good day. | 102

Words Read: _____
minus mistakes: _____
equals cwpm: _____

Phonics: CVC Short Pattern – Student Page 3

Peg had a wig. It was a big wig. It was a red	13
wig. Peg's wig was big and red. It covered her head.	24
Peg put her wig on top of her head.	33
Peg had a cat. Peg's cat was red. Peg's cat	43
matched her wig. It was funny to see a cat and a	55
wig the same.	58
Peg had a dog. Peg's dog was not red. Peg's	68
dog did not like the cat. Peg's dog hid from the	79
cat.	80
A rat bit Peg's cat. Peg took her cat to the	91
vet. The vet liked Peg's cat. The vet liked Peg's wig.	122
The dog stayed home.	126

Words Read: _____

minus mistakes: _____

equals cwpm: _____

Phonics: CVCC Short Vowel Pattern – Teacher Page

Word	Correct	Word	Correct
sand		tent	
hand		rent	
band		sent	
mask		went	
task		send	
lamp		lend	
ramp		bend	
fast		mend	
last		rest	
past		nest	
bank		send	
rank		desk	
vast		tend	

Short "a" (13)	Short "e" (13)

Phonics: CVCC Short Vowel Pattern – Student Page

Word	Word
sand	tent
hand	rent
band	sent
mask	went
task	send
lamp	lend
ramp	bend
fast	mend
last	rest
past	nest
bank	send
rank	desk
vast	tend

Phonics: CVCC Short Vowel Pattern

I have two hands.	4
I have two hands in the sand.	11
I have two hands.	15
I play in the band.	20
I put on a mask for the band.	28
The task at hand is to play for the band.	38
The band is last.	42
The band ranks last.	46
The band does not play in the sand.	54
The band plays fast.	58
There are many hands in the band.	65

Words Read: _____   minus mistakes: _____   equals cwpm: _____

Phonics: CVCC Short Vowel Pattern

I rest in the tent.	5
The tent is where I rest.	11
After I rest, I do my best.	18
I do my best after I rest.	25
I do my best after I rest in the tent.	85
I went to send the letter.	91
I went around the bend.	96
I went around the bend to send the letter.	105
I saw a nest.	110
I saw a nest around the bend.	117
I saw a nest around the bend as I sent a letter.	129

Words Read: _____ minus mistakes: _____ equals cwpm: _____

Phonics: CVCC Short Vowel Pattern

I need help.	3
I need help to bend.	8
I need help to bend and touch my toes.	17
I am on the mend.	122
I need rest; because, I am on the mend.	131
I can't bend; because, I am on the mend.	140
I bumped the desk.	144
I need help; because, I bumped the desk.	155
I need help to bend and to mend.	163
I mostly need rest.	167
If I rest, I will mend.	173

Words Read: _____ minus mistakes: _____ equals cwpm: _____

Phonics: CVCC Short Vowel Pattern

Go up the ramp.	4
See the lamp.	7
The lamp is up the ramp.	13
It is the last lamp on the street.	21
I went past the lamp.	26
I went past the lamp to send a letter.	35
I went past the bank.	40
I went past the bank to send a letter.	49
I went past the lamp to send a letter.	58
I got to the mailbox, but I did not have a stamp.	70
Please lend me a stamp, so I can send a letter.	81

Phonics: CVCC Short Pattern

Please give me a hand. Please give me a hand	10
moving the sand. We need to move the sand. It is	22
a task I need help with.	27
We have to move the sand. We have to	37
move the sand to make way for the band. The	48
band goes on the sand. The lamp goes on the sand.	59
The band and the lamp go on the sand.	66
The band will play under a tent. The tent goes	76
at the top of the ramp. I need help with the tent.	89
I need help with the tent after we move the sand.	99
The tent goes up last. The sand must be	109
moved first. First the sand, then the tent.	116
Thank you for your help.	121

Words Read: _____ minus mistakes: _____ equals cwpm: _____

Phonics: CVCC Short Pattern

Come here fast. We have a task at hand. I	10
need you fast to finish my task. We have to mend	22
the tent. We have to mend the tent fast.	31
After we mend the tent, we must send it to	41
the bank. Why send the tent to the bank? The	51
bank is using it for the parade. We will lend the	62
bank the tent for the parade.	68
If you help me fast, we can finish. If you help	78
me fast, we will finish the task.	86
After we mend the tent and send it to the	96
bank, we can rest.	100
Thank you for lending a hand.	106

Words Read: _____ minus mistakes: _____ equals cwpm: _____

Student: _____ Number: _____

Test 1 Date: _____ Test 2 Date: _____

Assessed for: _____ Letter Names _____ Letter sounds _____ Both

Phonics: CVCC Short Vowel Pattern

Word	Correct	Word	Correct
milk		pond	
silk		bond	
wilt		bulb	
sink		dump	
rink		lump	
risk		pump	
disk		must	
list		dust	
mist		bust	
wink		gulp	
pink		bunt	
wink		runt	
sock		just	

Short "i" (12)	Short "o" (3)	Short "u" (11)

Word	Word
milk	pond
silk	bond
wilt	bulb
sink	dump
rink	lump
risk	pump
disk	must
list	dust
mist	bust
wink	gulp
pink	bunt
soft	runt
sock	just

Phonics: CVCC Short Vowel Pattern

I gulp milk.	3
I gulp pink milk.	7
I gulp pink milk over the sink.	14
It is a risk to gulp milk.	21
It is a risk to gulp milk over the sink.	31
It is a risk to gulp milk because I can choke.	42
It is a risk to gulp pink milk over the sink.	53
If I don't gulp my milk, I will dump it out.	64
I don't want to dump my milk out.	72
I don't want to dump my pink milk out.	81
I don't want to dump my pink milk out in the sink.	93

Words Read: _____   minus mistakes: _____ equals cwpm: _____

Phonics: CVCC Short Vowel Pattern

The silk is soft.	4
The silk is pink.	8
The soft silk is pink.	13
The soft silk has a lump.	19
The lump is a big bump.	25
The lump is not a runt lump.	32
The lump must come off.	37
I see the lump under the bulb.	44
I see the silk lump under the light bulb.	53
The lump just must come off.	59
The silk is soft, but it has a lump	68

Words Read: _____ minus mistakes: _____ equals cwpm: _____

Name: _____ Number: _____

Phonics: CVCC Short Vowel Pattern

We must put it on the disk.	7
We must dump the dust.	12
We must dump the dust from the mist.	20
The rink is full of bumps.	26
The fish is a runt.	31
The fish in the pond is a runt.	39
The fish must not sink.	44
The pink flower will wilt.	49
We just finished our milk.	54
Put milk on the list.	59
We must put milk on the shopping list.	67

Words Read: _____ minus mistakes: _____ equals cwpm: _____

Name: _____ Number: _____

Phonics: CVCC Short Pattern

It is a risk to fish in the pond. The pond	11
water is dirty. We must pump the pond water. If	21
we pump the pond water, the plants will wilt. If we	32
don't pump the pond water, we can't fish. If we	42
pump the pond water, it will be cleaner.	50
It is on my list to pump the pond water. To	61
get to the pond, I walk by the dump. I head for	73
the pond. I walk past the dump. I get to the pond	85
and see the fish. The fish are runts. We must	95
pump the pond water so the fish will grow. The fish	106
are runts from the dirty water. The water is dirty	116
because it has not been pumped. It's now time to	126
pump the pond.	129

Words Read: _____ minus mistakes: _____ equals cwpm: _____

Phonics: CVCC Short Pattern

Please give me a hand. Please give me a hand	10
moving the sand. We need to move the sand.	19
Moving the sand is a task I need help with.	29
We have to move the sand. We have to	38
move the sand to make way for the band. The	48
band goes on the sand. The lamp goes on the sand.	59
The band and the lamp go on the sand.	68
The band will play under a tent. The tent goes	78
at the top of the ramp on the sand. I need help	90
with the tent after we move the sand.	98
The tent goes up last. The sand must be	107
moved first. First the sand, then ramp and finally	116
the tent. Thank you for your help.	123

Words Read: _____ minus mistakes: _____ equals cwpm: _____

Name: _____ Number: _____

Phonics: CVCC Short Pattern

We must learn to bunt. If we are to play ball, | 11

we must learn to bunt. Learning to bunt is on my | 22

list. Learning to bunt is on my list of things I must | 34

learn to do. | 37

The day I decided to learn to bunt is hot. The | 48

flowers wilt in the heat. There is no mist. I think of | 60

the cool pond. I think of learning to bunt. I would | 71

rather be at the pond. I would rather be at the | 82

pond than learning to bunt. | 87

The ball comes at me fast. It hits me. It makes | 98

a lump on my leg. It was a risk to learn to bunt. It | 112

was a risk and I got hit. I should have gone to the | 125

pond. | 126

Words Read: _____ minus mistakes: _____ equals cwpm: _____

Student: _____ Number: _____

Test 1 Date: _____ Test 2 Date: _____

Assessed for: _____ Letter Names _____ Letter sounds _____ Both

Phonics: CCVC Short Vowel Pattern

Word	Correct	Word	Correct
drag		slid	
flag		drop	
brag		plop	
plan		frog	
glad		stop	
slam		crop	
slab		drum	
sled		plum	
fled		club	
fret		grub	
swim		stub	
drip		slum	
trim		scum	

Short "a" (7)	Short "e" (3)	Short "i" (4)	Short "o" (5)	Short "u" (7)

Word	Word
drag	slid
flag	drop
brag	plop
plan	frog
glad	stop
slam	crop
slab	drum
sled	plum
fled	club
fret	grub
swim	stub
drip	slum
trim	scum

Name: _____ Number: _____

Phonics: CCVC Short Vowel Pattern

Do not drag the flag.	5
Do not drag the flag on the ground.	13
He will brag about the plan.	19
He will brag about the swim plan.	26
He will brag about the swim plan and be glad.	36
The flag is in the plan.	42
How is a flag in a swim plan?	50
Don't fret, the plan is sound.	56
I am glad he has a plan.	63
I am glad he has a swim plan.	71
I am not glad he will brag about the plan.	81

Words Read: _____ minus mistakes: _____ equals cwpm: _____

Name: _____ Number: _____

Phonics: CCVC Short Vowel Pattern

I will sled.	3
I will sled on the slab.	9
I will sled on the slab with Fred.	17
The frog sat on the plum.	23
The frog slid off the plum.	29
The drop was not part of his plan.	37
The frog did not want to slam into the slab.	47
The frog did slam into the slab.	54
The frog could not stop the drop.	61
It was a steep drop.	66
The frog was not glad he slid from the plum.	76

Words Read: _____   minus mistakes: _____ equals cwpm: _____

Phonics: CCVC Short Vowel Pattern

There is the club	4
Stop and listen to the drum.	10
The drum is beating in the club.	17
Let's go into the club.	22
We will eat some grub.	27
We will go to the club and eat some grub.	37
We will not stop there.	42
After the club, we'll go to the ice rink.	51
After the rink, we'll look for frogs.	58
After the frogs, we will eat plums.	65
The club, rink, grub and them plums, how fun.	74

Words Read: _____ minus mistakes: _____ equals cwpm: _____

Phonics: CCVC Short Pattern

You must not slam the flag. You must not slam	10
the flag on the ground. You must not drag the	20
flag. I am glad you are carrying the flag. Never	30
let the flag drag. Never let the flag slam or drag	41
on the ground.	44
You must carry the flag at the swim meet.	53
You must not drop the flag. You must stop if you	64
think you will drop the flag.	70
Fred will play the drum as you carry the flag.	80
You will stop in the center of the stands. Fred will	91
play his drum until you stop.	97

Words Read: _____

minus mistakes: _____

equals cwpm: _____

Phonics: CCVC Short Pattern

The boy rode the sled. The boy rode the sled	10
down the hill. He was glad to ride the sled. It was	22
his plan to ride the sled all day.	30
The boy was in a sled club. He was in a sled	42
club with lots of other boys and girls. The sled club	53
liked to sled. The sled club liked to plop their	63
toboggans down in the snow. The sled club also liked	73
to stop at the shop and eat plum ice cream.	83
"Don't fret," said the boy to his friends, "we	92
will stop sledding when it's dark, and then we will	102
get some grub."	105
"The grub we grab will be plum ice cream,"	114
said his friend.	117

Words Read: _____ minus mistakes: _____ equals cwpm: _____

Student: _____ Number: _____

Test 1 Date: _____ Test 2 Date: _____

Assessed for: _____ Short "a"   _____ fluency   _____both

Phonics: Short "a"

Word	Correct	Word	Correct
am		fat	
as		rat	
hand		mat	
ask		fad	
has		task	
camp		tan	
apple		plan	
at		man	
dad		ran	
had		fact	
sad		pan	
mad		fan	
cat		tad	

Short "a" (26)

Phonics: Short "a" – Student Page

Word	Word
am	fat
as	rat
hand	mat
ask	fad
has	task
camp	tan
apple	plan
at	man
dad	ran
had	fact
sad	pan
mad	fan
cat	tad

Name: _____ Number: _____

Phonics: Short "a" words

am	as	hand	ask	has	5
act	land	mad	has	camp	10
apple	at	sad	dad	had	15
am	as	hand	ask	has	20
act	land	mad	has	camp	25
apple	at	sad	dad	had	30
am	as	hand	ask	has	35
act	land	mad	has	camp	40
apple	at	sad	dad	had	45
am	as	hand	ask	has	50
act	land	mad	has	camp	55
apple	at	sad	dad	had	60
am	as	hand	ask	has	65
act	land	mad	has	camp	70
apple	at	sad	dad	had	75
am	as	hand	ask	has	80
act	land	mad	has	camp	85
apple	at	sad	dad	had	90
am	as	hand	ask	has	95
act	land	mad	has	camp	100
apple	at	sad	dad	had	105

Words Read: _____ minus mistakes: _____ equals cwpm: _____

Phonics: Short "a"

I am at camp.	4
I am at camp eating an apple.	11
I will ask dad.	15
I will ask dad for a cat.	22
I will ask dad for a mat.	29
I will ask dad for a cat and a mat.	39
I will ask dad for a fat cat.	47
I will ask dad for a fat cat and a mat.	58
I will be sad.	62
I will be said if dad says no.	70
I will be sad if dad says no to a cat.	82

Words Read: _____ minus mistakes: _____ equals cwpm: _____

Phonics: Short "a"

He has a rat.	4
His rat is mad	8
He has a mad rat.	13
It is a fact.	17
It is a fact he has a mad rat.	26
He has a plan.	30
He has a plan at hand.	36
His plan at hand is to have two rats.	45
His plan at hand is a tad silly.	53
Who wants two rats?	57
Whose plan at hand is to have two rats?	66

Words Read: _____ minus mistakes: _____ equals cwpm: _____

Name: _____ Number: _____

Phonics: Short "a"

Jan has a pan.	4
Jan has a tan pan.	9
Jan has a pan that is tan.	16
Jan's tan pan is a tad warm.	23
Jan used her tan pan.	28
Jan used her tan pan to cook for the man.	38
The man will ask for more food.	45
Jan will use her tan pan to cook more food.	55
Jan will use her tan pan to cook for the man.	65
The man will eat out of the tan pan.	74
The man will sit on a mat and eat out of the pan.	87

Words Read: _____ minus mistakes: _____ equals cwpm: _____

42

Name: _____ Number: _____

Phonics: Short "a" Words

Sam was at camp. This year, Sam liked camp very much. He | 12

never used to like camp. Every summer, Sam's dad dropped Sam | 23

off at camp. Every summer, Sam was sad to see his dad drive | 36

away. This year when dad left, Sam was not sad. | 46

"I am fine Dad," said Sam. | 52

"You're not sad?" asked Dad. | 57

"No," said Sam. "I am not sad. I am glad. I am glad to be at | 73

camp." | 74

"That's great," said Dad. | 78

"This camp has everything," Sam said. "We even have a band. | 89

Plus, did you know that the land my camp is on was once a fruit | 104

stand?" | 105

"You are acting so grown-up, Sam. I'm very proud of you," | 112

Dad smiled and waved. "Have fun at camp." | 120

"I will," said Sam. "I sure will." | 127

Words Read: _____ minus mistakes: _____ equals cwpm: _____

Student: _____ Number: _____

Test 1 Date: _____ Test 2 Date: _____

Assessed for: _____ Short "i" words _____ fluency _____both

Phonics: Short "i"

Word	Correct	Word	Correct
if		tip	
mix		hip	
fix		rig	
six		pit	
gift		fig	
lift		bit	
him		kit	
miss		fin	
milk		win	
flip		trim	
pig		slim	
sip		Jim	
rip		Kim	

Short "i" (26)

Phonics: Short "i" words– Student Page

Word	Word
if	tip
mix	hip
fix	rig
six	pit
gift	fig
lift	bit
him	kit
miss	fin
milk	win
flip	trim
pig	slim
sip	Jim
rip	Kim

Name: _____ Number: _____

Phonics: Short "i" Words

if	mix	fix	gift	miss	5
lift	him	six	milk	sip	10
pig	sip	tip	rip	flip	15
if	mix	fix	gift	miss	20
lift	him	six	milk	sip	25
pig	sip	tip	rip	flip	30
if	mix	fix	gift	miss	35
lift	him	six	milk	sip	40
pig	sip	tip	rip	flip	45
if	mix	fix	gift	miss	50
lift	him	six	milk	sip	55
pig	sip	tip	rip	flip	60
if	mix	fix	gift	miss	65
lift	him	six	milk	sip	70
pig	sip	tip	rip	flip	75
if	mix	fix	gift	miss	80
lift	him	six	milk	sip	85
pig	sip	tip	rip	flip	90
if	mix	fix	gift	miss	95
lift	him	six	milk	sip	100
pig	sip	tip	rip	flip	105

Words Read: _____ minus mistakes: _____ equals cwpm: _____

Name: _____ Number: _____

Phonics: Short "i"

Jim has a pig named Kim.	5
Jim feeds his pig milk.	10
Jim's pig will enter a milk drinking contest.	18
The pig will win the contest.	23
Jim's pig, named Kim, will win the contest.	31
The pig named Kim is trim.	37
The pig named Kim is slim.	43
Jim will fix the trim pig her breakfast.	51
Jim will fix a bit of pig food for her breakfast.	62
Jim will also fix his pig her milk.	70
The trim pig is hip and will win the contest.	80

Words Read: _____ minus mistakes: _____ equals cwpm: _____

Phonics: Short "i"

The figs are in the pit.	6
There are six are figs in the pit.	14
Jim tipped the tree.	18
Jim tipped the tree and the figs fell.	26
Jim tipped the tree and the figs fell into the pit.	37
Jim will miss the figs.	42
Jim will miss the figs in the pit.	51
Jim flipped when the figs fell.	57
Jim flipped at the tipped tree.	63
There will be no more figs.	69
The six figs in the pit are out of reach.	79

Words Read: _____ minus mistakes: _____ equals cwpm: _____

Name: _____ Number: _____

Phonics: Short "i" Words

Hil got a gift. The gift was a pig. Hil named the pig. Hill named   15

the pig Miss Priss.   19

It was a special pig. If Hil gave the pig a big donut, the pig   34

would flip. The pig flipped for donuts. It was a silly pig.   46

One day when Hil gave Miss Priss a donut, the pig flipped. The   58

pig flipped and ripped the chair cushion.   65

Hil did not know what to do. Mom would be mad. Mom would   78

be mad the pig ripped the cushion. The pig was not to be in the   93

house. The pig was six feet long. The pig was too big to be   107

flipping in the house.   111

Hil lifted up the chair. Hil lifted up the chair to see if she   125

could fix the rip. The rip was big. The rip was big, but it could be   141

fixed.   142

Hil took a sip of milk and fixed the rip. The pig watched.   155

Words Read: _____ minus mistakes: _____ equals cwpm: _____

Assessed for: _____ Short "u" words _____ fluency _____both

Phonics: Short "u" words

Word	Correct	Word	Correct
up		pup	
us		rut	
duck		dug	
luck		sum	
bus		bud	
hunt		hut	
nut		mutt	
bump		jug	
shut		cut	
gum		cup	
hug		tub	
pug		rub	
run		bun	

Short "u" (26)

Phonics: Short "u" words– Student Page

Word	Word
up	pup
us	rut
duck	dug
luck	sum
bus	bud
hunt	hut
nut	mutt
bump	jug
shut	cut
gum	cup
hug	tub
pug	rub
run	bun

Name: _____ Number: _____

Phonics: Short "u" Words

up	us	duck	luck	bus	5
hunt	mud	bump	nut	gum	10
hug	pug	run	pup	rut	15
up	us	duck	luck	bus	20
hunt	mud	bump	nut	gum	25
hug	pug	run	pup	rut	30
up	us	duck	luck	bus	35
hunt	mud	bump	nut	gum	40
hug	pug	run	pup	rut	45
up	us	duck	luck	bus	50
hunt	mud	bump	nut	gum	55
hug	pug	run	pup	rut	60
up	us	duck	luck	bus	65
hunt	mud	bump	nut	gum	70
hug	pug	run	pup	rut	75
up	us	duck	luck	bus	80
hunt	mud	bump	nut	gum	85
hug	pug	run	pup	rut	90
up	us	duck	luck	bus	95
hunt	mud	bump	nut	gum	100
hug	pug	run	pup	rut	105

Words Read: _____   minus mistakes: _____   equals cwpm: _____

Phonics: Short "u"

The pup is up.	4
The pup is up in the cup.	11
The pup is a mutt.	16
The pup in the cup is a mutt.	24
The pup in the cup is a pug.	32
The pug likes ducks.	36
The pug likes to hunt ducks.	42
The pup in the cup likes to hunt.	50
The pug in the cup likes to hunt ducks.	59
The pup in the cup will run to the ducks.	60
The pup in the cup is named Bud.	77

Words Read: _____ minus mistakes: _____ equals cwpm: _____

Phonics: Short "u"

The jug is full of gum.   6

The cup is full of nuts.   12

I dug the nuts from the ground.   19

The bus took me to the hut.   26

By the hut, were the nuts.   32

I dug the nuts by the hut.   39

The mutt had a cut.   44

The mutt had a cut from the tub.   52

The mutt rubbed his cut.   57

The mutt rubbed his cut from the tub.   65

The mutt chewed the jug full of gum.   73

Words Read: _____ minus mistakes: _____ equals cwpm: _____

Name: _____ Number: _____

Phonics: Short "u" Words

My dog is Gus. My dog is a pug. My dog, Gus, is a pug.   116

My dog Gus likes to hunt. My dog Gus likes to hunt ducks.   28

My dog Gus and I take the bus. Gus and I take the bus   43

to hunt ducks. We hunt ducks and then we feed them nuts.   55

Gus likes to find the ducks. He runs like a pup. Gus is not   69

a pup. Gus is an old dog. Gus is an old dog who likes to   84

chase ducks.   86

We are going to a new hunting spot. The bus bumps   97

along. The bus bumps along until it gets us to our new spot.   110

The bumpy bus hits many ruts. The ruts are deep and send   122

us up from our seats. I hug tightly onto Gus. He does not   135

like the bus. He does not like the ruts. He does not like the   149

bumpy, rutty ride. He does like the nuts.   157

We get to our stop. We see the ducks. Gus runs to   169

them. I throw the nuts. We have a great time.   179

Words Read: _____ minus mistakes: _____ equals cwpm: _____

Student: _____ Number: _____

Test 1 Date: _____ Test 2 Date: _____

Assessed for: _____ Short "e" words _____ fluency _____both

Phonics: Short "e" words

Word	Correct	Word	Correct
end		pet	
well		let	
send		set	
help		get	
went		leg	
mess		beg	
next		bed	
less		hen	
tell		when	
bell		step	
den		sped	
fed		stem	
met		deck	

Short "e" (26)

Phonics: Short "e" words– Student Page

Word	Word
end	pet
well	let
send	set
help	get
went	leg
mess	beg
next	bed
less	hen
tell	when
bell	step
den	sped
fed	stem
met	deck

Name: _____ Number: _____

Phonics: Short "e" Words

end	well	send	help	went	5
mess	next	less	tell	bell	10
den	fed	met	pet	let	15
end	well	send	help	went	20
mess	next	less	tell	bell	25
den	fed	met	pet	let	30
end	well	send	help	went	35
mess	next	less	tell	bell	40
den	fed	met	pet	let	45
end	well	send	help	went	50
mess	next	less	tell	bell	55
den	fed	met	pet	let	60
end	well	send	help	went	65
mess	next	less	tell	bell	70
den	fed	met	pet	let	75
end	well	send	help	went	80
mess	next	less	tell	bell	85
den	fed	met	pet	let	90
end	well	send	help	went	95
mess	next	less	tell	bell	100
den	fed	met	pet	let	105

Words Read: _____ minus mistakes: _____ equals cwpm: _____

Name: _____ Number: _____

Phonics: Short "e"

He met the pet.	4
Jeff met the pet.	8
The pet was a mess.	13
The pet was a mess and begged for help.	22
The pet needed to be fed.	28
Jeff sent for the hen.	33
The hen had food for the pet.	40
The hen had food for the pet?	47
The hen's food was wet.	52
The hen was not the pet.	58
The hen fed the pet food that was wet.	67

Words Read: _____ minus mistakes: _____ equals cwpm: _____

Name: _____ Number: _____

Phonics: Short "e"

He will send the bell.   5

Tell him to send the bell.   11

I will help him send the bell.   18

I will get the bell.   23

The bell is over the bed.   29

Tell him the bell is hanging over the bed.   38

Step on the bed to get the bell.   46

Step your leg up to the bed.   53

Step your leg up to the bed and get the bell.   64

The bell fell from the bed to the floor.   73

Help me pick it up and get it sent.   82

Words Read: _____ minus mistakes: _____ equals cwpm: _____

Name: _____ Number: _____

Phonics: Short "e" Words

Let me tell you a story about my pet. The story is about my | 14

pet and his bell. The story about my pet does not end well. | 26

My pet is a jet-black cat named Ted. Ted used to wear a | 40

bell. The bell was less for noise and more for show. Ted loved his | 54

bell. I could tell Ted loved his bell. I could tell Ted loved his bell | 69

very much. | 71

One day, after he was fed, Ted let out a meow. I ran to | 85

Ted. He was a mess. Next to Ted was the bell with a broken | 99

ribbon. Ted was sad. I could tell, but then he ate the bell. Ted ate | 114

the bell. I listened to his belly. I could not hear the bell. | 127

I took Ted to the vet. The vet said Ted would have to stay | 141

overnight. The vet made my pet stay overnight. The vet fed Ted. | 153

He helped Ted feel better. He helped Ted get rid of the bell. | 166

When I went to pick up Ted, the bell was gone. | 177

end	well	send	help	went	182
mess	next	less	tell	bell	187
den	fed	met	pet	let	192

Words Read: _____ minus mistakes: _____ equals cwpm: _____

Student: _____ Number: _____

Test 1 Date: _____ Test 2 Date: _____

Assessed for: _____ Short "o" words _____ fluency _____ both

Phonics: Short "o" words

Word	Correct	Word	Correct
on		got	
odd		pot	
lot		not	
spot		dot	
stop		hot	
rocks		jog	
socks		pop	
box		rot	
fox		cod	
dog		rod	
hop		nod	
fog		drop	
mop		glob	

Short "o" (26)

Phonics: Short "o" Words– Student Page

Word	Word
on	got
odd	pot
lot	not
spot	dot
stop	hot
rocks	jog
socks	pop
box	rot
fox	cod
dog	rod
Hop	nod
fog	drop
mop	glob

Phonics: Short "o"

The box is on top. | 5

The box is on top of the pot. | 13

The box is on top of the pot with spots. | 23

The pot has spots. | 27

The fox and the dog see the box. | 34

The fox and the dog see the box on top. | 44

The fox and the dog see the box on top of the pot. | 57

The dog and the fox hop up to the top. | 67

The dog and the fox hop up to the box. | 77

The dog and the fox hop up to the pot with spots. | 89

The fox and the dog drop the box from the pot. | 100

Words Read: _____ minus mistakes: _____ equals cwpm: _____

Phonics: Short "o"

Bob nods.	2
Bob nods at the pot.	7
Bob nods at the hot pot.	13
The hot pot is odd.	18
The hot pot is full of cod.	25
The hot pot is odd and full of cod.	34
The odd hot pot is full of cod.	42
The cod is for Pop.	47
Pop likes to eat cod.	52
Pop likes to eat cod after an evening jog.	61
Pop likes to eat hot cod after his evening jog.	71

Words Read: _____ minus mistakes: _____ equals cwpm: _____

Name: _____ Number: _____

Phonics: Short "o" Words

on	odd	lot	spot	stop	5
rocks	socks	box	fox	dog	10
fog	hop	mop	got	pot	15
on	odd	lot	spot	stop	20
rocks	socks	box	fox	dog	25
fog	hop	mop	got	pot	30
on	odd	lot	spot	stop	35
rocks	socks	box	fox	dog	40
fog	hop	mop	got	pot	45
on	odd	lot	spot	stop	50
rocks	socks	box	fox	dog	55
fog	hop	mop	got	pot	60
on	odd	lot	spot	stop	65
rocks	socks	box	fox	dog	70
fog	hop	mop	got	pot	75
on	odd	lot	spot	stop	80
rocks	socks	box	fox	dog	85
fog	hop	mop	got	pot	90
on	odd	lot	spot	stop	95
rocks	socks	box	fox	dog	100
fog	hop	mop	got	pot	105

Words Read: _____ minus mistakes: _____ equals cwpm: _____

Phonics: Short "o" Words

I have an odd dog. My odd dog sleeps in a box. My odd dog | 15

wears socks. My odd dog sleeps in a box and wears socks. It is | 30

odd to see a dog in socks. It is not odd to see a dog in a box. | 49

My odd dog's box is also full of rocks. Now, that is odd. | 60

My dog's best friend is a fox. The fox lives under a rock. | 74

The fox stops to see my dog a lot. | 82

One day, it was foggy, and my dog hopped out the door. I | 96

was mopping the floor. I was using a pot of water. I did not see | 111

that my dog got away. He went to see his friend the fox. He | 126

went to see his friend the fox and brought back new rocks. | 136

He put the rocks in his box. My dog put the rocks in his box | 151

and changed his socks. | 155

We cleaned the pot and made popcorn in it. I told my dog | 169

to stop visiting the fox in the fog without me. | 178

on	odd	lot	spot	stop	183
rocks	socks	box	fox	dog	188
fog	hop	mop	got	pot	193

Words Read: _____ minus mistakes: _____ equals cwpm: _____

Student: _____ Number: _____

Test 1 Date: _____ Test 2 Date: _____

Assessed for: _____ "th" words _____ fluency _____ both

Phonics: "th" words – Teacher Page

Word	Correct	Word	Correct
than		father	
that		tooth	
them		teeth	
then		thick	
these		path	
those		moth	
think		the	
there		fifth	
bath		sixth	
with		other	
third		three	
both		booth	
mother		Ruth	

"th" (26)

Phonics: "th" words– Student Page

Word	Word
than	father
that	tooth
them	teeth
then	thick
these	path
those	moth
think	the
there	fifth
bath	sixth
with	other
third	three
both	booth
mother	Ruth

Name: _____   Number: _____

Phonics: Words with "th"

than	that	them	then	these	5
those	think	bath	both	with	10
there	cloth	thin	third	mother	15
than	that	them	then	these	20
those	think	bath	both	with	25
there	cloth	thin	third	mother	30
than	that	them	then	these	35
those	think	bath	both	with	40
there	cloth	thin	third	mother	45
than	that	them	then	these	50
those	think	bath	both	with	55
there	cloth	thin	third	mother	60
than	that	them	then	these	65
those	think	bath	both	with	70
there	cloth	thin	third	mother	75
than	that	them	then	these	80
those	think	bath	both	with	85
there	cloth	thin	third	mother	90
than	that	them	then	these	95
those	think	bath	both	with	100
there	cloth	thin	third	mother	105

Words Read: _____   minus mistakes: _____ equals cwpm: _____

70

Phonics: Words with "th"

It is this or that?	5
It is these or those?	10
That is Ruth's tooth.	14
I think that is Ruth's tooth.	20
I think that is Ruth's father.	26
I think that is Ruth's father with her tooth.	35
Ruth's father and mother both have teeth.	42
Ruth lost a tooth.	46
I think that is Ruth's tooth her father has.	55
Ruth's mother does not have Ruth's tooth.	62
Ruth's tooth is with her father.	68

Words Read: _____ minus mistakes: _____ equals cwpm: _____

Phonics: Words with "th"

Watch this.	2
Watch this moth.	5
Watch this moth think it can fly.	12
Watch that moth.	15
Watch that other moth take a bath.	22
The bath is on the path.	28
This is the path.	32
This is the moth's bath path.	38
The moth will take a bath.	44
Wait, that moth can't take a bath.	51
Moth's do not take baths.	56

Words Read: _____ minus mistakes: _____ equals cwpm: _____

Name: _____ Number: _____

Phonics: Words with "th"

Mother and father sit outside. They sit outside and watch the | 11

birds. They sit outside and watch the birds take a bath. | 22

Mother and father watch them more than usual. They love | 32

these birds. This is the third day. This is the third day they watch | 45

the birds. This is the third day they watch the birds take a bath. | 59

Mother is thin. Father is not thin. Mother is thankful father | 71

is not thin. He keeps them both warm when they sit outside. | 82

I asked my mother and father if I could sit with them. I asked | 96

to sit with them and watch the bath too. | 105

They let me sit with them. I was thankful to sit with them. I | 119

was thankful to watch the birds. I was thankful to watch the birds | 132

take a bath. | 135

It is fun to sit with them. My mother and father are fun to | 149

sit with, and the bird are fun to watch. | 158

than	that	them	then	these	163
those	think	bath	third	with	168
there	thank	thin	father	mother	173

Words Read: _____ minus mistakes: _____ equals cwpm: _____

Student: _____ Number: _____

Test 1 Date: _____ Test 2 Date: _____

Assessed for: _____ "sh" words _____ fluency _____both

Phonics: Words with "sh"

Word	Correct	Word	Correct
shell		shirts	
ship		should	
shop		shade	
she		shake	
sheep		brush	
shut		bush	
shape		sharp	
dish		shine	
fish		show	
wish		crash	
rush		cash	
short		mash	
shoe		stash	

"sh" (26)

74

Phonics: Words with "sh"

Word	Word
shell	shirts
ship	should
shop	shade
she	shake
sheep	brush
shut	bush
shape	sharp
dish	shine
fish	show
wish	crash
rush	cash
short	mash
shoe	stash

Name: _____   Number: _____

Phonics: Words with "sh"

shell	ship	shop	she	sheep	5
shut	shape	dish	fish	wish	10
rush	short	shoe	shirt	shut	15
shell	ship	shop	she	sheep	20
shut	shape	dish	fish	wish	25
rush	short	shoe	shirt	shut	30
shell	ship	shop	she	sheep	35
shut	shape	dish	fish	wish	40
rush	short	shoe	shirt	shut	45
shell	ship	shop	she	sheep	50
shut	shape	dish	fish	wish	55
rush	short	shoe	shirt	shut	60
shell	ship	shop	she	sheep	65
shut	shape	dish	fish	wish	70
rush	short	shoe	shirt	shut	75
shell	ship	shop	she	sheep	80
shut	shape	dish	fish	wish	85
rush	short	shoe	shirt	shut	90
shell	ship	shop	she	sheep	95
shut	shape	dish	fish	wish	100
rush	short	shoe	shirt	shut	105

Words Read: _____   minus mistakes: _____   equals cwpm: _____

Phonics: Words with "sh"

She has a shell.	4
She has a shell in the shape of two sheep.	14
She has a shell in the shape of a fish.	24
She has shells in the shape of fish and sheep.	34
She is on a ship.	39
She is on a ship in shorts.	46
She is on a ship with bare feet.	54
She is on a ship in shorts and no shoes.	64
She will shop on the ship.	70
She will shop on the ship for a dish.	79
She'll shop on the ship for a dish for her shells.	90

Words Read: _____ minus mistakes: _____ equals cwpm: _____

Phonics: Words with "sh"

The show is in the shade.	6
The brush is in the paint.	12
We should wear shiny shirts.	17
She is sharp.	20
She has a stash of cash.	26
She has a stash of cash for sheep.	34
She has a stash of cash for new shoes.	43
She has three short wishes.	48
We are in a rush to wish.	55
We are in a rush to wish on shiny stars.	65
We will show you how to wish.	72

Words Read: _____ minus mistakes: _____ equals cwpm: _____

Phonics: Words with "sh"

I went to the shore. I went to the shore to pick up shells. | 15

the shore I saw some sheep. The sheep were shut up in a pen. A | 30

farmer was feeding the sheep. The sheep had a dish the shape | 43

of a star. The sheep were in a rush to eat. | 53

I went to the shore. I went to the shore and saw some fish. | 67

The fish were in a rush to get to their food. Everything at the | 81

shore was eating. | 84

I went to the shore. I went to the shore without any food. I | 98

wish I had shopped for food. All of this eating is making me want | 112

to eat. | 114

The sheep have their food. The fish have their food. I have | 126

my shells. I don't have any food. I did not shop for food. | 139

I have my shoes. I have my shirt. I wish I had food. | 152

shell	ship	shop	she	sheep	157
shut	shape	dish	fish	wish	162
rush	short	shoe	shirt	shut	167

Words Read: _____ minus mistakes: _____ equals cwpm: _____

Student: _____ Number: _____

Test 1 Date: _____ Test 2 Date: _____

Assessed for: _____ "st" words _____ fluency _____both

Phonics: Words with "st"

Word	Correct	Word	Correct
stand		fast	
still		stump	
stamp		last	
stick		rust	
stone		nest	
stop		stack	
rest		cast	
must		star	
just		store	
story		story	
stem		stay	
last		stack	
best		stuff	

"st" (26)

Phonics: Words with "st"

Word	Word
stand	fast
still	stump
stamp	last
stick	rust
stone	nest
stop	stack
rest	cast
must	star
just	store
story	story
stem	stay
last	stack
best	stuff

Name: _____ Number: _____

Phonics: Words with "st"

stand	stamp	stick	stone	stop	5
still	stump	fast	last	best	10
rest	must	just	story	stem	15
stand	stamp	stick	stone	stop	20
still	stump	fast	last	best	25
rest	must	just	story	stem	30
stand	stamp	stick	stone	stop	35
still	stump	fast	last	best	40
rest	must	just	story	stem	45
stand	stamp	stick	stone	stop	50
still	stump	fast	last	best	55
rest	must	just	story	stem	60
stand	stamp	stick	stone	stop	65
still	stump	fast	last	best	70
rest	must	just	story	stem	75
stand	stamp	stick	stone	stop	80
still	stump	fast	last	best	85
rest	must	just	story	stem	90
stand	stamp	stick	stone	stop	95
still	stump	fast	last	best	100
rest	must	just	story	stem	105

Words Read: _____ minus mistakes: _____ equals cwpm: _____

Name: _____ Number: _____

Phonics: Words with "st"

Stand still.	2
Stand still and the rest will go fast.	10
Stand still and I will tell you a story.	19
Stand still and look at the nest.	26
Stand still and look at the nest, please.	34
You must stand still to hear the story.	42
You must stand still to see the nest.	50
The story is about the nest.	56
Once I begin, the story will go fast.	64
You are standing still.	68
I will now tell you my story.	75

Words Read: _____ minus mistakes: _____ equals cwpm: _____

Phonics: Words with "st"

Stop talking.	2
Stop talking so fast.	6
Stop stacking.	8
Stop stacking the dishes.	12
Stop stacking the dishes so fast.	18
Stop talking until you start your story.	25
You tell the best stories.	30
Stop stacking the dishes and tell your story.	38
I'll stop talking, so you can start your story.	47
I love your stories.	51
I'll stop talking and listen now.	57

Words Read: _____ minus mistakes: _____ equals cwpm: _____

Name: _____ Number: _____

Phonics: Words with "st"

I have a story. I have a story about a stem. I have a story   15

about a stump. I have a story about a stem and a stump.   28

A large stump stood by a stone. The stone was the throne   40

of a fairy. The fairy was the last of her kind.   51

One day, the fairy was sitting on the stone. She was sitting   63

on the stone to rest. She must have just sat down, when the stem   77

of a flower fell on her head.   84

"Ouch," she said.   87

The stem stood. The fairy was startled.   94

"I am a magic stem," it said.   101

"Oh," said the last fairy.   106

"I have a wand. My wand is a stick. I will grant you a wish."   121

The fairy thought for a moment and then wished for a   132

better story.   134

stand	stamp	stick	stone	stop	139
still	stump	fast	last	best	144
rest	must	just	story	stem	149

Words Read: _____ minus mistakes: _____ equals cwpm: _____

Student: _____ Number: _____

Test 1 Date: _____ Test 2 Date: _____

Assessed for: _____ long "a" words _____ fluency _____both

Phonics: Words with long "a" – Teacher Page

Word	Correct	Word	Correct
name		skate	
same		mate	
came		rate	
game		gate	
save		case	
brave		fade	
face		base	
place		gave	
race		lake	
pace		wade	
snake		day	
wake		say	
bake		play	

Long "a" (26)

Phonics: Words with long "a"

Word	Word
name	skate
same	mate
came	rate
game	gate
save	case
brave	fade
face	base
place	gave
race	lake
pace	wade
snake	day
wake	say
bake	play

Name: _____ Number: _____

Phonics: Words with long "a"

name	same	came	game	save	5
brave	face	place	race	pace	10
snake	wake	bake	skate	mate	15
name	same	came	game	save	20
brave	face	place	race	pace	25
snake	wake	bake	skate	mate	30
name	same	came	game	save	35
brave	face	place	race	pace	40
snake	wake	bake	skate	mate	45
name	same	came	game	save	50
brave	face	place	race	pace	55
snake	wake	bake	skate	mate	60
name	same	came	game	save	65
brave	face	place	race	pace	70
snake	wake	bake	skate	mate	75
name	same	came	game	save	80
brave	face	place	race	pace	85
snake	wake	bake	skate	mate	90
name	same	came	game	save	95
brave	face	place	race	pace	100
snake	wake	bake	skate	mate	105

Words Read: _____   minus mistakes: _____   equals cwpm: _____

Name: _____ Number: _____

Phonics: Words with long "a"

Name the game.   3

Name the same game.   7

Name the skating game.   11

Name the place with the gate.   17

The lake is home base.   22

Save me a place.   26

Save me a place to bake a cake.   34

I see your face.   38

Wade into the lake.   42

I gave my mate my place.   48

Name a brave mate who stole home plate.   56

Phonics: Words with long "a"

There are three streets.   3

The three streets are green.   8

There are three green streets.   13

Please feed the seal.   17

The seal seems hungry.   21

You will each feed the seal cream.   28

You will each play on the same team.   36

You will each eat a meal.   42

Each team will eat an easy meal.   49

It is my dream to have ice cream.   57

The sea is deep and green.   63

Words Read: _____ minus mistakes: _____ equals cwpm: _____

Name: _____ Number: _____

Phonics: Words with long "a"

My name is Kate. I like to race. I like to race on my skates.   15

My name is Kate and I like to race on my skates.   27

    I keep a fast pace. I keep a fast pace on my skates. I am   42

brave on my skates. I skate with my mates.   51

    One day we decided to bake a cake. We decided to bake a   67

cake rather than skate. We baked our cake in the shape of a   90

snake. It is the same cake that we baked last year. We saved the   104

recipe.   105

    This year the cake had a funny face. We did everything the   116

same, but the face was not the same. The face did not turn out   130

the same, but the cake tasted delicious   138

    We ate our cake and then went out to skate. We went out   151

to skate at a very fast pace.   158

name	same	came	game	save	163
brave	face	place	race	pace	168
snake	wake	bake	skate	mate	173

Words Read: _____ minus mistakes: _____ equals cwpm: _____

Student: _____ Number: _____

Test 1 Date: _____ Test 2 Date: _____

Assessed for: _____ long "e" words _____ fluency _____both

Phonics: Words with long "e"

Word	Correct	Word	Correct
three		seem	
agree		each	
feel		easy	
need		sea	
street		feed	
beat		deep	
easy		leak	
each		meal	
dream		heap	
cream		seal	
green		east	
mean		seat	
team		seen	

Long "e" (26)

Phonics: Words with long "e"

Word	Word
three	seem
agree	each
feel	easy
need	sea
street	feed
beat	deep
easy	leak
each	meal
dream	heap
cream	seal
green	east
mean	seat
team	seen

Name: _____ Number: _____

Phonics: Words with long "e"

three	agree	feel	need	street	5
beat	easy	each	dream	green	10
mean	team	bean	queen	seem	15
three	agree	feel	need	street	20
beat	easy	each	dream	green	25
mean	team	bean	queen	seem	30
three	agree	feel	need	street	35
beat	easy	each	dream	green	40
mean	team	bean	queen	seem	45
three	agree	feel	need	street	50
beat	easy	each	dream	green	55
mean	team	bean	queen	seem	60
three	agree	feel	need	street	65
beat	easy	each	dream	green	70
mean	team	bean	queen	seem	75
three	agree	feel	need	street	80
beat	easy	each	dream	green	85
mean	team	bean	queen	seem	90
three	agree	feel	need	street	95
beat	easy	each	dream	green	100
mean	team	bean	queen	seem	105

Words Read: _____ minus mistakes: _____ equals cwpm: _____

Phonics: Words with long "e"

Once upon a time there were three queens. The three	10
queens lived on the same street. The three queens had green	21
houses. The three queens liked to eat beans.	29
Two of the queens were nice. Once of the queens was mean.	41
Two of the queens agreed to be on the same team. The team was	54
to pick up trash. The third queen did not agree.	65
"Queens should not pick up trash," the third queen said.	75
"But it is easy to do," the second queen said.	85
"And if we each help, our street will stay clean," the first	97
queen said.	99
"I do not like this team," said the third queen.	109
She went to her green home. She looked out her window.	120
She saw the other two queens. They were laughing. The team	131
looked fun. The mean queen finally joined the team. By helping	142
the team, she was not mean anymore.	149

three	agree	feel	need	street	154
beat	easy	each	dream	green	159
mean	team	bean	queen	seem	164

Words Read: _____ minus mistakes: _____ equals cwpm: _____

Student: _____ Number: _____

Test 1 Date: _____ Test 2 Date: _____

Assessed for: _____ end in "y" _____ fluency _____both

Phonics: Words that end in "y"

Word	Correct	Word	Correct
any		busy	
many		cozy	
very		rosy	
pretty		mommy	
funny		daddy	
sorry		jelly	
money		party	
happy		tardy	
story		tiny	
every		ruby	
penny		fancy	
sunny		scary	
baby		runny	

End in "y" (26)

Phonics: Words that end in "y"

Word	Word
any	busy
many	cozy
very	rosy
pretty	mommy
funny	daddy
sorry	jelly
money	party
happy	tardy
story	tiny
every	ruby
penny	fancy
sunny	scary
baby	runny

Name: _____   Number: _____

Phonics: Words that end in "y"

any	many	very	pretty	funny	5
sorry	money	happy	story	every	10
penny	sunny	baby	busy	cozy	15
any	many	very	pretty	funny	20
sorry	money	happy	story	every	25
penny	sunny	baby	busy	cozy	30
any	many	very	pretty	funny	35
sorry	money	happy	story	every	40
penny	sunny	baby	busy	cozy	45
any	many	very	pretty	funny	50
sorry	money	happy	story	every	55
penny	sunny	baby	busy	cozy	60
any	many	very	pretty	funny	65
sorry	money	happy	story	every	70
penny	sunny	baby	busy	cozy	75
any	many	very	pretty	funny	80
sorry	money	happy	story	every	85
penny	sunny	baby	busy	cozy	90
any	many	very	pretty	funny	95
sorry	money	happy	story	every	100
penny	sunny	baby	busy	cozy	105

Words Read: _____   minus mistakes: _____   equals cwpm: _____

Name: _____ Number: _____

Phonics: Words that end in "y"

My pretty mommy makes jelly.	5
The baby had a runny nose.	11
Mommy and daddy have runny noses.	17
Mommy and daddy are very busy.	23
It is a happy story.	28
It is a happy story about jelly.	35
It is a happy story about a baby who eats jelly.	46
The ruby was fancy.	50
The party was cozy.	54
A penny is money.	58
Are any busy people tardy?	63

Words Read: _____ minus mistakes: _____ equals cwpm: _____

Phonics: Words that end in "y"

We have many funny stories.	5
We have fancy homes.	9
Our homes are fancy and cozy.	15
I am sorry you missed the party.	22
I am sorry your baby has a runny nose.	31
She is very rosy.	35
Every person at the party liked scary stories.	43
He is a happy, pretty person.	49
I have money.	52
He is tiny	55
She is scary, and he is tiny.	62

Words Read: _____ minus mistakes: _____ equals cwpm: _____

Phonics: Words that end in "y"

There once was a pretty baby. The baby was also funny. The	12
pretty baby was funny. The baby was pretty, funny and happy.	23
When it was sunny the baby went outside. The baby went	34
outside with her mommy. Every sunny day was a happy day. The	46
baby and her mommy would be busy all day long. The mommy	58
would tell funny stories. The baby would laugh. The baby would	69
laugh very hard.	72
The mommy and the baby stayed in, all cozy, on cold days.	84
There were not many cozy days. The mommy was not sorry there	96
were not many cozy days. The mommy liked sunny days. The	107
mommy liked telling stories, outside, on sunny days.	115
The baby and the mommy were happy. They were happy for	126
sunny days. They were happy for funny stories. They were happy	137
for sunny days and funny stories.	143

Words Read: _____   minus mistakes: _____   equals cwpm: _____

any	many	very	pretty	funny	147
sorry	money	happy	story	every	152
penny	sunny	baby	busy	cozy	157

Student: _____ Number: _____

Test 1 Date: _____ Test 2 Date: _____

Assessed for: _____ words with "ch" _____ fluency _____both

Phonics: Words with "ch"

Word	Correct	Word	Correct
chin		child	
chip		chest	
chap		touch	
chat		much	
ranch		punch	
chop		reach	
lunch		ranch	
chick		such	
check		rich	
inch		witch	
pinch		ditch	
chain		match	
chew		batch	

Words with "ch" (26)

Phonics: Words with "ch"

Word	Word
chin	child
chip	chest
chap	touch
chat	much
ranch	punch
chop	reach
lunch	ranch
chick	such
check	rich
inch	witch
pinch	ditch
chain	match
chew	batch

Name: _____ Number: _____

Phonics: Words With "ch"

chin	chip	chop	chap	ranch	5
lunch	chick	check	inch	pinch	10
chest	child	chair	chain	chew	15
chin	chip	chop	chap	ranch	20
lunch	chick	check	inch	pinch	25
chest	child	chair	chain	chew	30
chin	chip	chop	chap	ranch	35
lunch	chick	check	inch	pinch	40
chest	child	chair	chain	chew	45
chin	chip	chop	chap	ranch	50
lunch	chick	check	inch	pinch	55
chest	child	chair	chain	chew	60
chin	chip	chop	chap	ranch	65
lunch	chick	check	inch	pinch	70
chest	child	chair	chain	chew	75
chin	chip	chop	chap	ranch	80
lunch	chick	check	inch	pinch	85
chest	child	chair	chain	chew	90
chin	chip	chop	chap	ranch	95
lunch	chick	check	inch	pinch	100
chest	child	chair	chain	chew	105

Words Read: _____ minus mistakes: _____ equals cwpm: _____

Phonics: Words with "ch"

Keep your chin up.   4

The chap kept his chin up.   10

Chat with the child.   14

Chat with the child about chewing his food.   22

Chat with the child about ditching the batch.   30

He is rich.   33

The chick is at the ranch.   39

We had lunch in the ditch.   45

The chain was on her chest.   51

The check for lunch came.   56

We had punch for lunch.   61

Words Read: _____ minus mistakes: _____ equals cwpm: _____

Phonics: Words with "ch"

Sit on the chair and chat.	6
Sit on the chair and chat with the chap.	15
Reach for the batch of cookies.	21
Chew your food.	24
Pinch the chopstick between your fingers.	30
Reach for the chair.	34
The witch had lunch with her broom.	41
The child chopped the tree.	46
It was too much to touch.	52
It was too much to touch the chick.	60
It was too much to reach the spoon.	68

Words Read: _____ minus mistakes: _____ equals cwpm: _____

Name: _____ Number: _____

Phonics: Words With "ch"

"Chew your chop," said the boy to his chum.   9

"I like to swallow it whole," said the chum.   18

"Not healthy" replied the boy, "you should chew your chop."   28

"On the ranch, we did not chew our chops," said the chum.   40

The ranch was far away. The chum was in town to buy chicks.   53

He needed chicks and chains. The chains were for his door. He   65

needed his chains one inch each. The chum brought his child with   77

him. The child was a funny chap. The child did not chew his chop   91

either.   92

"We don't chew chops," said the child. "That is not the way   104

of the ranch."   107

They finished lunch, paid the bill and left for the store. They   119

got the chicks and the chains, then they went for ice cream.   131

chin	chip	chop	chap	ranch	136
lunch	chick	check	inch	pinch	141
chest	child	chair	chain	chew	146

Words Read: _____ minus mistakes: _____ equals cwpm: _____

Student: _____ Number: _____

Test 1 Date: _____ Test 2 Date: _____

Assessed for: _____ words with long "i" _____ fluency _____both

Phonics: Words with long "I"

Word	Correct	Word	Correct
shine		child	
bride		idea	
mine		silent	
time		spied	
dime		bike	
like		find	
line		while	
dive		tiger	
die		right	
lie		five	
sigh		lime	
fright		nine	
might		light	

Words with long "i" (26)

Word	Word
shine	child
bride	idea
mine	silent
time	spied
dime	bike
like	find
line	while
dive	tiger
die	right
lie	five
sigh	lime
fright	nine
might	light

Name: _____   Number: _____

Phonics: Words With long "i"

shine	bride	mine	time	dime	5
like	line	dive	die	lie	10
sigh	fright	might	child	idea	15
silent	spied	bike	find	while	20
tiger	right	five	lime	nine	25
shine	bride	mine	time	dime	30
like	line	dive	die	lie	35
sigh	fright	might	child	idea	40
silent	spied	bike	find	while	45
tiger	right	five	lime	nine	50
shine	bride	mine	time	dime	55
like	line	dive	die	lie	60
sigh	fright	might	child	idea	65
silent	spied	bike	find	while	70
tiger	right	five	lime	nine	75
shine	bride	mine	time	dime	80
like	line	dive	die	lie	85
sigh	fright	might	child	idea	90
silent	spied	bike	find	while	95
tiger	right	five	lime	nine	100
shine	bride	mine	time	dime	105

Words Read: _____   minus mistakes: _____   equals cwpm: _____

Phonics: Words with long "I"

The dime had a bright shine.	6
The shine was bright.	10
The bike had a bright shine.	16
The dime and the bike had shine.	23
The bride might fight.	27
The bride might fight for sunlight.	33
The sunlight might be bright.	38
The bride likes bright sunlight.	43
The bride will wed in bright sunlight.	50
The bride will ride a bike.	56
The bride will ride a bike in the bright sunlight.	66

Words Read: _____   minus mistakes: _____   equals cwpm: _____

Phonics: Words with long "i"

The child had an idea.	6
The child had a bright idea.	15
The child's bright idea was to find a tiger.	21
The tiger would give the child a fright.	24
The child liked frights.	30
The child tried with all his might to find a tiger.	34
The child was silent, and the tiger was silent.	41
It was right past five when the tiger arrived.	46
The tiger arrived by the lime tree.	52
The child was frightened by the tiger.	60
The idea to find a tiger worked.	68

Words Read: _____ minus mistakes: _____ equals cwpm: _____

Phonics: Words With long "i"

I am going to ride my bike. I am going to ride my bike in the   16

light. The light is bright, when I ride my bike. I ride silently down   30

the center line.   33

The time goes by. The time goes by when I ride my bike. I   47

ride to my cousin Mike's house. Mike's house is easy to find. It is   61

number 9 Dine Road.   65

Mike likes to ride bikes, too. We ride until we spy a dry fly.   79

We find the fly diving for a candy wrapper.   88

We turn right and ride. We turn right and ride under a   100

bright sky. We ride quietly under the bright sky. We stop at the   113

park. We stop at the park in time to see five kites. The five   127

kites fly. The five kites dive. We watch for a while.   138

At nine minutes to five, we get on our bikes. We get on   151

our bikes and ride home.   156

Words Read: _____   minus mistakes: _____equals cwpm: _____

Student: _____ Number: _____

Test 1 Date: _____ Test 2 Date: _____

Assessed for: _____ words with long "o"   _____ fluency   _____ both

Phonics: Words with long "o"

Word	Correct	Word	Correct
row		window	
sow		impose	
go		total	
no		hotel	
rose		grow	
nose		slow	
hose		snow	
code		arrow	
cone		below	
mole		pillow	
note		yellow	
goat		mope	
oak		spoke	

Words with long "o" (26)

Word	Word
row	window
sow	impose
go	total
no	hotel
rose	grow
nose	slow
hose	snow
code	arrow
cone	below
mole	pillow
note	yellow
goat	mope
oak	spoke

Phonics: Words With long "o"

row	sow	go	no	rose	5
nose	hose	code	cone	mole	10
note	goat	oak	window	impose	15
total	hotel	grow	slow	snow	20
arrow	below	pillow	yellow	mope	25
spoke	pillow	yellow	below	hotel	30
row	sow	go	no	rose	35
nose	hose	code	cone	mole	40
note	goat	oak	window	impose	45
total	hotel	grow	slow	snow	50
arrow	below	pillow	yellow	mope	55
spoke	pillow	yellow	below	hotel	60
row	sow	go	no	rose	65
nose	hose	code	cone	mole	70
note	goat	oak	window	impose	75
total	hotel	grow	slow	snow	80
arrow	below	pillow	yellow	mope	85
spoke	pillow	yellow	below	hotel	90
row	sow	go	no	rose	95
nose	hose	code	cone	mole	100
note	goat	oak	window	impose	105

Words Read: _____ minus mistakes: _____ equals cwpm: _____

Phonics: Words with long "o"

Joe will go.	3
Joe will go to the snow.	9
Joe found a rose.	13
Joe found a rose in the snow.	20
Roses don't grow in the snow.	26
Joe saw a mole.	30
Joe saw a mole in the snow.	37
The mole was near the rose.	43
The mole's nose was gold.	48
Joe wrote a note about the nose.	55
Joe wrote a note about the gold nose.	63

Words Read: _____ minus mistakes: _____ equals cwpm: _____

Phonics: Words with long "o"

Open the window.	3
Go open the window slowly.	8
Don't impose on the girls.	13
They are throwing arrows.	17
They are throwing arrows at pillows.	23
The pillows were under the oak.	29
We are going to the hotel.	35
We spoke to the hotel owner.	41
The hotel was yellow.	45
The yellow hotel had big windows.	51
The goat had a big nose.	57

Words Read: _____ minus mistakes: _____ equals cwpm: _____

Name: _____ Number: _____

Phonics: Words With long "o"

Joe and Mo liked to row. Joe and Mo liked to go row their	14
boat under the river oaks. The oaks shaded the slow river. Mo	26
and Joe could only go to the river when the flow was slow.	39
Joe and Mo also rowed on a team. The team rowed all over	53
the world. Joe and Mo were spokesmen for the rowing team. They	65
wore their yellow jerseys and spoke of rowing.	73
Joe and Mo had a rowing code. The rowing code was to	85
never row alone. Rowing alone could be dangerous.	93
Joe and Mo told their team to row together. Joe and Mo	105
told their team to never row alone. Joe and Moe made their	117
team take notes. The notes were about: never rowing alone, how	128
to row fast, and how to row slow. They also spoke about how to	142
avoid oak roots in the slow river.	149
Joe and Mo's team was very successful at rowing. They had	160
a total of 12 awards.	165

Words Read: _____ minus mistakes: _____ equals cwpm: _____

Student: _____ Number: _____

Test 1 Date: _____ Test 2 Date: _____

Assessed for: _____ words with long "u"   _____ fluency   _____both

Phonics: Words with long "u"

Word	Correct	Word	Correct
use		unit	
cube		student	
cute		unicorn	
dude		rude	
duke		rule	
fuse		duty	
huge		tune	
glue		ruin	
mute		fluid	
due		cruse	
clue		flute	
blue		mule	
juice		dune	

Words with long "u" (26)

Phonics: Words with long "u"

Word	Word
use	unit
cube	student
cute	unicorn
dude	rude
duke	rule
fuse	duty
huge	tune
glue	ruin
mute	fluid
due	cruse
clue	flute
blue	mule
juice	dune

Phonics: Words With long "u"

use	cube	cute	dude	duke	5
fuse	huge	glue	mute	due	10
clue	blue	juice	unit	student	15
unicorn	rude	rule	duty	tune	20
ruin	fluid	cruise	flute	mule	25
dune	student	clue	dune	due	30
use	cube	cute	dude	duke	35
fuse	huge	glue	mute	due	40
clue	blue	juice	unit	student	45
unicorn	rude	rule	duty	tune	50
ruin	fluid	cruise	flute	mule	55
dune	student	clue	dune	due	60
use	cube	cute	dude	duke	65
fuse	huge	glue	mute	due	70
clue	blue	juice	unit	student	75
unicorn	rude	rule	duty	tune	80
ruin	fluid	cruise	flute	mule	85
dune	student	clue	dune	due	90
use	cube	cute	dude	duke	95
fuse	huge	glue	mute	due	100
clue	blue	juice	unit	student	105

Words Read: _____ minus mistakes: _____ equals cwpm: _____

Phonics: Words with long "u"

Use the cube, dude.	3
The duke used the cube to tube.	9
The duke liked to tube on the river.	13
The duke liked to tube on the huge tube.	20
I don't have a clue how to tube.	26
Dude, how do you tube?	30
The blue tube was due.	37
The blue tube was due back to the rental place.	43
It was the dukes duty to return the tube.	48
The cute duke used the cubed tube.	55
The duke drake juice after tubing.	63

Words Read: _____ minus mistakes: _____ equals cwpm: _____

Phonics: Words with long "u"

The student read the unit.	3
The unit was about rude unicorns.	8
The student read the unit about rude unicorns.	13
The dude went on a cruise.	17
The dude took a cruise.	23
The cruise had one rule.	29
The cruise rule was that no flutes were allowed.	35
The cruise had a rude rule.	41
Why no flutes on the cruise?	45
The mule lived on the dune.	51
The mule lived on the huge dune.	57

Words Read: _____ minus mistakes: _____ equals cwpm: _____

Phonics: Words With long "u"

The Duke of Glue was a sticky mess. Why? The duke's duty	14
was to make the glue to stick the rulers together. Due to the	26
rules of the kingdom, the glue had to be blue.	39
Every day, the Duke of Glue went to the huge factory by	53
mule. The factory was huge, but the décor was cute. The duke	65
loved his job. The duke refused to let the mess bother him.	73
People from all over the kingdom, from the dunes to the	85
ancient ruins loved the way the duke ruled. Very few understood	93
why the duke ran the glue factory. They also wondered why the	105
rulers had to stick together.	117
The duke hired a cute flute player to welcome people to the	128
factory. He also gave them juice. His subjects loved the catchy	142
tune. They loved the sticky duke. Mostly, they loved the duty the	149
duke felt to the people he ruled.	160
	165

Words Read: _____ minus mistakes: _____ equals cwpm: _____

Fluency Record

Name: _____ Period: _____

Passage #	DATE	CWPM	DATE	CWPM	DATE	CWPM	DATE	CWPM	DATE	CWPM
CVC 1										
CVC 2										
CVC 3										
CVCC 4										
CVCC 5										
CVCC 6										
CVCC 7										
CVCC 8										
CVCC 9										
CVCC 10										
CVCC 11										
Short "a" 12										
Short "I" 13										
Short "u" 14										
Short "e" 15										
Short "o" 16										
"th" 17										
"sh" 18										

Passage #	DATE	CWPM	DATE	CWPM	DATE	CWPM	DATE	CWPM	DATE	CWPM
"st" – 19										
Long "a" 20										
Long "e" 21										
End in "y" 22										
"ch" 23										
Long "I" 24										
Long "o" 25										
Long "u" 26										

Phonics Practice for Older Students

ISBN-13 : 979-8370715815

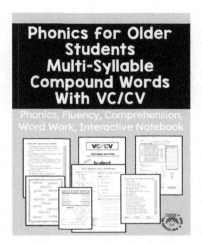

ISBN-13 : 979-8370873805

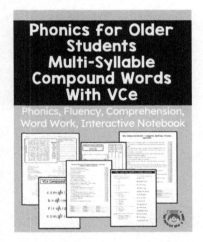

ISBN-13 : 979-8367292787

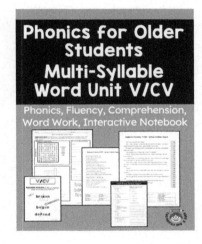

ISBN-13 : 979-8367258271

Phonics Practice for Older Students

This series contains phonics and multi-syllable word practice for older struggling readers. Perfect for older students who lack the necessary decoding and word skills to read fluently but need practice that does not look primary. Engaging age-appropriate work that helps build confidence and fluent readers at their level - both in look and content.

The resources in this series are based on the body of research that incorporates insights and research psychology, educational psychology, cognitive science, and cognitive neuroscience that states that one of the key elements in successful reading instruction for struggling older reluctant readers is the incorporation of age-appropriate systematic and explicit phonics into instructional practices.

Made in the USA
Las Vegas, NV
04 December 2024